Book

of

Yakub

Father of the Caucasian Race

2nd Edition

By Rasheed L. Muhammad

Table of Contents

Forward

In 1934 the Honorable Elijah Muhammad published a Weekly News Paper, *The Final Call To Islam.*

The forward of this book will contain an article he wrote August 18, 1934—Detroit, Mich. His article was headlined: "A Warning To The Black Man Of America."

Bible Nothing But Warning to Black Man of America

The whole contents of the Bible that you have, predict the return of us back to Islam and Asia, our home. But remember that the same devils who enslaved our forefathers and ourselves DILUTED THE TRUTH IN THE BIBLE. When they translated it out of the Greek tongues into English language. It was originally given to Hebrews by Ethiopians (Moslems). The Asiatic Moslems knew that they would have a lost brother somewhere on the Planet Earth. But the Holy Quran did not say where he would be. But they all believed that in the devil's civilization was where their lost brother would be. So they gave this warning Book (Book) to the Jews (devils) that perchance if the lost brother would see it and read and understand its contents he would rise from the death of ignorance to the call of the Messenger (Prophet Fard Mohammed) whom Allah would send before the destruction of his enemies (Malachi 4:5).

The Bible is Diluted

Therefore when our enemies understood that the Book was for us they slew every one of the Translators of the Bible as it was then in its truest sense. They finally got a bunch of wicked translators and through them they took out some of the truth and added lies to some parts of it. And that part which they did publish was put in symbolic language words. So obscure is the truth in the American Bible that it took no less that the Saviour of the Lost Brother of Asia to unfold its contents. But Glory to Prophet Fard Mohammed, our Redeemer, whom Allah has sent, and made the hidden truth plain to us, that we may teach it to our brothers who are blind to it and are sleeping in the grave of North America....

Chapter One

The Man Yakub

According the teachings of the Honorable Elijah Muhammad, the man Yakub lived 6,600 years ago in the holy land of the east. Yakub lived to be 150 years of old. He is hidden in the Christian Bible under the name Jacob. This man opposed the righteous government of his day. In the book of Genesis 32, the righteous government is symbolically hidden under the name angel.

The ancient black people of Egypt referred to Yakub's people as Sea People.

"...the Sea Peoples are described and depicted on reliefs at Medinet Habu and Karnak (*Caucasian to Right*) as well as the Great Harris Papyrus, a list of temple endowments in the reign of Rameses III (1184-1153 BC). The latter sources indicate that the Sea Peoples were not simply engaged in random acts of plundering but were part of a significant movement of displaced peoples migrating into Syria-Palestine and Egypt. It is clear that they planned to settle in the areas that they attacked, since they are portrayed not merely as armies of warriors but also as whole families bringing their possessions with them in ox-drawn carts…[1]

The Christian bible symbolically hid Yakub's made man or race or people under the name Caphtorites coming out from Caphtor (Crete). These people entered parts of the holy land thousands of years ago to destroy it. [Deutoromny 2:23] *"And as for the Avvites who lived in villages as far as Gaza, the Caphtorites coming out from Caphtor destroyed them and settled in their place."*

Ancient black Hebrews describe these people by a name that would translate as "The Invaders," or, less harsh, "The Immigrants." Caphtorites a people a-kin to the Philistines were not and are not the original

---

[1] http://www.ancient-egypt.co.uk/people/pages/sea_people.htm

black inhabitants of the holy land i.e., Mecca, Egypt, Gaza or Jerusalem. [Genesis 10:14]

"In 135 AD, the Roman Emperor Hadrian, after putting down the rebellion of Simon bar-Chochva, deported all the Jews *en masse* from the region (the Diaspora) and renamed it Palaestina, a Latinized version of the Hebrew *philistim*."[2] Is this one reason why the name *Philistine* in Hebrew means *philisth or* "invasion" or "inroad" or "intrusion." Scholars say it was used not as a native name for a people, but a descriptive name. All original natives of ancient Palestine were Asiatic black men, women and children.

Of course, the above history is a late part of the history about how Yakub's people entered into the holy land 2,000 years before Prophet Moses (Musa) was born. The missing history is as follows:

"Six thousand years ago, or to be more exact 6,600 years ago, as Allah taught me, our nation gave birth to another God whose name was Yakub. He started studying the life germ of man to try making a new creation (new man)...

"According to the word of Allah to me, Mr. Yakub was seen by the twenty-three Scientists of the black nation, over 15,000 years ago. They predicted that in the year 8,400 (that was in our calendar year before this world of the white race), this man (Yakub) would be born

[2] http://archaeologynewsnetwork.blogspot.com/2010/05/philistines.html#.UXH1ynjD_IU

twenty miles from the present Holy City, Mecca, Arabia. And, that at the time of his birth, the satisfaction and dissatisfaction of the people would be: -- 70 per cent satisfied, 30 per cent dissatisfied...

"...Mr. Yakub was, naturally, born out of the 30 per cent dissatisfied. As we know, wherever there is a longing or demand for a change, nature will produce that man, who will bring it about.

"Allah taught me that the present percentage of dissatisfaction is 98 per cent near, 100 per cent, with the present ruling powers. This 100 per cent dissatisfied will bring about a 100 per cent change. Yakub did not bring about a 100 per cent change, but near (90 per cent)...

"...the boy Yakub, first came into the knowledge of just who he was -- born to make trouble, break peace, kill and destroy his own people with a made enemy to the black nation....

"...Yakub was the founder of unlike attracts and like repels, though Mr. Yakub was a member of the black nation. He began school at the age of four. He had an unusual sized head. When he had grown up, the others referred to him as the Big head scientist.

"At the age of 18 he had finished all of the colleges and universities of his nation, and was seen preaching on the streets of Mecca, making converts. He made such impressions on the people that many began following him.

"He learned from studying the germ of the black man, under the microscope, that there were two people in him, and that one was black, the other brown.

"He said if he could successfully separate the one from the other he could graft the brown germ into its last stage, which would be white. With his wisdom, he could make the white, which he discovered was the weaker of the black germ (which would be unalike) rule the black nation for a time (until a greater one than Yakub was born)..." [3]

While Yakub was exiled on Patmos (Pelan), he wrote about the Greater One in Bible Revelations 12:5. Since he did know what his name would be, Yakub referred to the Greater One as a *"male child, who will rule all the nations with an iron scepter...snatched up to God and to his throne."* Yakub opens his book of Revelation with these words, *"I, John, your brother and partner in the tribulation and the kingdom and the patient endurance that are in Jesus, was on the island called Patmos on account of the word of God and the testimony of Jesus.* (Revelations 1:9) But before his kingdom could be fully manifested and governed by his new race, the black nation (people) had to be put to sleep spiritually, mentally and morally. And so it began.

---

[3] Message To The Blackman Chapter 55, "Making of the Devil, by Elijah Muhammad, Messenger of Allah

"As Mr. Yakub continued to preach for converts, he told his people that he would make the others work for them. (This promise came to pass). Naturally, there are always some people around who would like to have others do their work. Those are the ones who feel for Mr. Yakub's teaching, 100 per cent.[4]

Notice here how the 30% dissatisfied did not want to work, but wanted others to do their work. Wasn't this the reason for servants on the Arabian Peninsula? Wasn't this the reason for the Slave Trade in North America? What is relevant here is why and how Europe's elite or wanna-be elite felt it necessary to enslave the dark nations of the earth by hook or crook. They sought someone else to do their work for free or cheap, which helped their society to become so rich and powerful with every natural resource humans need stolen from third world nations.

It's no coincidence the Christian Bible [2 Thessalonians 2:8-9] says *"8 And then shall that Wicked be revealed, whom the Lord shall consume with the spirit of his mouth, and shall destroy with the brightness of his coming: 9 Even him, whose coming is after the working of Satan with all power and signs and lying wonders...,"*

Technically speaking, the empire that Yakub's people ultimately built ended in 1914 AD as a result of World War I (WWI) and mismanagement of their monetary system. Without a true monetary system, you have no real commercial civilization. The current

[4] Message To The Blackman Chapter 55, "Making of the Devil, by Elijah Muhammad, Messenger of Allah

system governing you and I today is called legal fiction under the guise of the United States—A Federal Corporation.[5]

Brittan and America (Manasseh and Ephraim)

"The most perfect monetary system humans have yet created was the world gold standard system of the late 19th century, roughly 1870-1914....

"...By 1910, most countries in the world officially had "monometallic" monetary systems, with gold alone as the standard of currency value. This eliminated many of the difficulties of bimetallic systems, which had caused minor but chronic problems in the earlier 19th century...

"... In the United States in 1910, gold bullion reserve coverage was 42% of banknotes in circulation..."[6]

In a book written by Authur Bloomfield entitled, *Monetary Policy Under the International Gold Standard: 1880-1914.* It was published in 1959. Bloomfield provides references to major central bank balance sheets around the world. He summarizes various "reserve ratios," but includes not only gold bullion but also foreign exchange reserves (i.e., bonds denominated in foreign gold-linked currencies). The "reserve ratios," on this basis for 1910, were 46% in

---

[5] **28 USC § 3002 - Definitions - Legal Information Institute**

[6] http://www.forbes.com/sites/nathanlewis/2013/01/03/the-1870-1914-gold-standard-the-most-perfect-one-ever-created/

Britain, 54% in Germany, 60% in France, 41% in Belgium, 73% for the Netherlands, 68% for Denmark, 80% for Finland, 75% for Norway, 75% for Switzerland, 55% for Russia, and 62% for Austro-Hungary. Reserve ratios for gold bullion alone would be, naturally, less than these numbers...The pre-1914 era was the age of empire, and many of these countries were formally or informally within one or another European empire...if not for World War I [in 1914], the rise of Keynesian notions...floating currency... their catastrophic failure – it will be very easy to create, once again, a superlative world gold standard system...

Of course this will be accomplished, but not under the rulership of Yakub's people. Their 6,000 years ended in 1914. This year is equal to the Original Asiatic Calendar (AOC) Master W. Fard Muhammad made known to the Honorable Elijah Muhammad and the lost and found Nation of Islam regarding the time given to Yakub's people i.e., year *9*,000 to year 15,000 = 6,000 years. This also demonstrates that it took the white man 5,956 years to figure out how to perfect a commercial gold standard monetary system from the time they left Patmos with specific instructions to rule over land, sea and original people [**Matthew 23:15**]. Consequently we equate the above AOC years to the Christian calendar *in that* year 15,000 is equivalent with the Christian year 1914. You see, they were barely out of the 19th century and merely 14 years into the 20th century. In other words, for 44 years [1870 + 44 = 1914], they were able to enjoy a perfected monetary system under international commercial law created by white people for them. But thereafter, it all came crashing down. Did Yakub foresee this too? YES! Revelations 18, 19 and 20 symbolically reveal the end times of their vile civilization strictly governed under "white authority".

In fact, Yakub did not see his people in power beyond the 21st and 22nd century. By the time he begins to envision, in Revelations 21 and 22, the True and Faithful is transitioning His righteous civilization back into power and authority

"In the Book of Revelations, we are given 22 closing chapters which sum up the collective work of the angels in announcing the Presence of God and that of His Christ in this ending Hour."[7]

I ask, is it a coincidence that Yakub (John the Revelator) began seeing and writing about his visions from the *9th verse of Revelations* one? Could this number 9 represent year *9*,000 as taught by the Honorable Elijah Muhammad? Then, *Revelation chapter 16* describes the final seven Vials of the wrath of God, representing the climax of God's punishment of sinners during the Tribulation period. No repentance is invited or shown.

---

[7] http://www.finalcall.com/artman/publish/Columns_4/article_9379.shtml

[Revelation 16:16-21] *"16 **Then they gathered the kings together to the place that in Hebrew is called Armageddon.**" 17 The seventh angel poured out his bowl into the air, and out of the temple came a loud voice from the throne, saying, "It is done!" 18 Then there came flashes of lightning, rumblings, peals of thunder and a severe earthquake. No earthquake like it has ever occurred since mankind has been on earth, so tremendous was the quake. 19 The great city split into three parts, and the cities of the nations collapsed. God remembered Babylon the Great and gave her the cup filled with the wine of the fury of his wrath. 20 Every island fled away and the mountains could not be found. 21 From the sky huge hailstones, each weighing about a hundred pounds, fell on people. And they cursed God on account of the plague of hail, because the plague was so terrible."*

"The rule of the White race terminates at the *16,000th year* and that year is the beginning of the Black Nation's rule again, as we ruled before the 9,000th year of Yakub's making. This is the beginning of what is prophesied—the 7,000th year, meaning the 7,000th year after the rule of 6,000 years by the White race, and in our calendar history, it is the *16,000th year* (this is called the 7,000th year by the Christian writers).

"There is much more on this subject that I would like to teach and write, but the space is limited."[8]

---

[8] Our Saviour Has Arrived, Chapter 23, By Elijah Muhammad

Chapter Two

Jesus Encounters Yakub's People

The Christian Bible clearly states by one man came sin and death [Romans 5:17] *"It is certain that death ruled because of one person's failure. It's even more certain that those who receive God's overflowing kindness and the gift of his approval will rule in life because of one person, Jesus Christ."* This man represents Yakub along with the 30% dissatisfied. Conversely, the good news is the person referred to as Christ was born 6,563 after Yakub. His name, we now know is Master W. Fard Muhammad. He is the Finder of the Lost and Found members of the Nation of Islam in North America. The Honorable Elijah Muhammad was taught by Him face to face, the following history:

"...when this man is born (Yakub), he will change civilization (the world), and produce a new race of people, who would rule the original black nation for 6,000 years (from the nine thousandth year to the fifteen thousandth year).

"After that time, the original black nation would give birth to one, whose wisdom, Knowledge and power would be infinite. One, whom the world would recognize as being the greatest and mightiest God, since the creation of the universe. And, that He would destroy Yakub's world and restore the original nation, or ancient nation, into power to rule forever.

"This mighty One is known under many names. He has no equal. There never was one like Him. He is referred to in the Bible as God Almighty, and in some places as Jehovah, the God of Gods, and the Lord of Lords.

"The Holy Quran-an refers to Him as Allah, the One God; beside Him, there is no God and there is none like Him; the Supreme Being; the mighty, the wise, the best knower; the light; the life giver; the Mahdi...

"He, also, referred to as the Christ, the second Jesus. The Son of Man, who is wise and is all-powerful. He knows how to reproduce the universe, and the people of His choice. He will remove and destroy the present, old warring wicked world of Yakub (the Caucasian world) and set up a world of peace and righteousness, out of the present so-called Negroes, who are rejected and despised by this world."[9]

When Rome ruled the known world, the "first" Jesus of 2,000 years ago learned about Yakub's principal ruling stock when he addressed them in chapter 8 in the bible book of John.

[31] **To the Jews who had believed him**, *Jesus said, "If you hold to my teaching, you are really my disciples. 32 Then you will know the truth, and the truth will set you free."* [33] *They answered him,* **"We are Abraham's descendants and have never been slaves of anyone. How can you say that we shall be set free?"** [34] *Jesus replied, "Very truly I tell you, everyone who sins is a*

---

[9] Message To The Blackman Chapter 55, "Making of the Devil, by Elijah Muhammad, Messenger of Allah

slave to sin. 35 Now a slave has no permanent place in the family, but a son belongs to it forever. 36 So if the Son sets you free, you will be free indeed. 37 I know that you are Abraham's descendants. Yet you are looking for a way to kill me, because you have no room for my word. 38 I am telling you what I have seen in the Father's presence, and you are doing what you have heard from your father." ³⁹ "Abraham is our father," they answered. **"If you were Abraham's children," said Jesus, "then you would do what Abraham did.** *40 As it is, you are looking for a way to kill me, a man who has told you the truth that I heard from God. Abraham did not do such things. 41 You are doing the works of your own father." "We are not illegitimate children," they protested. "The only Father we have is God himself." ⁴² Jesus said to them, "If God were your Father, you would love me, for I have come here from God. I have not come on my own; God sent me. 43 Why is my language not clear to you? Because you are unable to hear what I say. 44* **You belong to your father, the devil, and you want to carry out your father's desires. He was a murderer from the beginning, not holding to the truth, for there is no truth in him. When he lies, he speaks his native language, for he is a liar and the father of lies...."**

During this debate, ask yourself what religious text was the Jews reading differently from the one Jesus studied wherein they missed [Genesis 15:13-15] *"Then the LORD said to him, "Know for certain that for four hundred years your descendants will be strangers in a country not their own and that they will be enslaved and mistreated there. ¹⁴ But I will punish the nation they serve as slaves, and afterward they will come out with great* *possessions.* Was the Jewish leadership, back then, living under the influence or doctrine of the Babylonian Talmud? Emphatically yes!

"The Rabbis tell us that the authority of the Talmud (and therefore their authority), is derived from God Himself....directly to Moses.

"'Moses passed it on to Joshua. Joshua gave it to the Elders. The Elders gave it to the Prophets, and the Prophets gave to the Men of the Great Assembly'

"The Rabbis tell us that Talmud divinely supplements Torah or teaches us of things that the Torah fails to mention....And if they don't follow Talmud, it is seen as sin.[10]

The Islamic book of scripture, Holy Quran, does not mention Talmud. However, it does mention Torah. *"Surely We sent down the Torah, wherein is guidance and light; thereby the Prophets who had surrendered themselves gave judgment for those of Jewry, as did the masters and the rabbis, following such portion of God´s Book as they were given to keep and were witnesses to. So fear not men, but fear you Me; and sell not My signs for a little price. Whoso judges not according to what God has sent down - they are the unbelievers."* (Qur'an 5:44)

---

[10] Ariel & Devorah Berkowitz, Torah Rediscovered (Lakewood, CO: First Fruits of Zion, 1996), p. 81. This is from the Mishna, tractate Pirke Avot 1:1.

"The title "Rabbi" was borne by the sages of ancient Israel, who were ordained by the Sanhedrin [supreme Jewish religious body with arrest powers during time of Jesus] in accordance with the custom handed down by the elders. They were titled *Ribbi* and received authority to judge penal cases. *Rab* was the title of the Babylonian sages who taught in the Babylonian academies."[11]

As it were, 400 years before the birth of Jesus, the Babylonian Talmud was in existence. For all intent and purpose, Jewish Rabbis (spiritual and legal leadership) were given a choice to abide by Torah (Old Testament) or live by the Talmud. It appears that 2,000 years ago, Talmudic literature dominated their way of thinking; their way of governing their religious socio-economic kingdom. Naturally, it is/was in contradiction to the righteous governments. So I think it is safe to conclude, Jesus of 2,000 years ago eventually saw this and that with his own eyes.

Jesus taught real peace, he was a true black man of Asia. He had hair like lamb's wool and feet like brass burned in an oven as describes in Revelations 1:14. Was Jesus' truth partially rejected due his black skin? Definitely yes!

"The black nation is only fooling themselves to take the Caucasian race otherwise. This is what Jesus learned of

---

[11] http://en.wikipedia.org/wiki/Rabbi#Historical_overview

their history, before He gave up His work of trying to convert the new or white race to the religion of Islam.

"And, the same knowledge of them was given to Muhammad by the Imams (or scientists) of Mecca. That is why the war of the Muslims against them came to a stop.

"Muhammad was told that he could not reform the devils and that the race had 1,400 more years to live; the only way to make righteous people (Muslims) out of them was to graft them back into the black nation.

"This grieved Muhammad so much that it caused him heart trouble until his death (age sixty-two and one half years). The old scientists used to laugh at Muhammad for thinking that he could convert them (the devils) to Islam. This hurt his heart."[12]

In others words, Prophet Muhammad of Arabia, was made very aware of his open disputers and how their preordained time to rule had not concluded. So when did the Muslims stop warring against the disputers? Around 836 years after Jesus was rejected and crucified and 118 plus years after Prophet Muhammad's passing away (PBUH). So let's us see.

"When the Abbasid Caliphate *[Founded by the descendants of the Prophet Muhammad's youngest uncle, Abbas ibn Abd al-Muttalib born 566–653 AD]*

---

[12] Message To The Blackman Chapter 55, "Making of the Devil, by Elijah Muhammad, Messenger of Allah

shifted its capital to Baghdad, the centre of learning, gradually moved to the Abbasid capital in 750 AD, which became in due course the heir of Athens and Alexandria as the new cultural metropolis of the medieval world. About two centuries later Cordoba, capital of Muslim Spain, began to vie with Baghdad as the centre of 'ancient learning'. From Cordoba, Greek-Arabic philosophy and science were transmitted across the Pyrenees to Paris, Bologna and Oxford in the twelfth and the thirteenth centuries.

"The initial reception of Greek-Hellenistic philosophy in the Islamic world was mixed. It was frowned upon at first as being suspiciously foreign or pagan, and was dismissed by conservative theologians, legal scholars and grammarians as pernicious or superfluous. By the middle of the eighth century AD the picture had changed somewhat, with the appearance of the rationalist theologians of Islam known as the **Mu'tazilites**, who were thoroughly influenced by the methods of discourse or dialectic favoured by the Muslim philosophers. Of those philosophers, the two outstanding figures of the ninth and tenth centuries were al-Kindi and al-Razi, who hailed Greek philosophy as a form of liberation from the shackles of dogma or blind imitation (taqlid). For al-Kindi, the goals of philosophy are perfectly compatible with those of religion, and, for al-Razi, philosophy was the highest expression of man's intellectual ambitions and the noblest achievement of that noble people, the

Greeks, who were unsurpassed in their quest for wisdom (hikma).[13]

Once we actually understand the whys and wherefores of the Abbasid Dynasty, it becomes very clear what Elijah Muhammad wrote in 1960 during the month of December in the Muhammad Speaks Newspaper Vol. 1, No. 4 ***"If Islam had been forced upon all the people of the earth during the past 6000 years there would not have been any 'world of Christianity,' there would not have been any 'World of Buddhism,'...and there would never have been anything like 'The Caucasian World.' Islam would have prevented their progress. God Himself has held Islam 'in check' to these other 'world' free reign during the past 6,000 years."***

[13] http://en.wikipedia.org/wiki/Abbasid_Caliphate

Chapter Three

Let Us Make Man

What Master W. Fard Muhammad revealed to the Honorable Elijah Muhammad concerning Yakub grafting the white race is a must review. He revealed:

"As he (Yakub) made converts in and around the Holy City of Mecca, persecutions set in. The authorities became afraid of such powerful teachings, with promises of luxury and making slaves of others. As they began making arrests of those who believed the teaching, the officers would go back and find, to their surprise, others still teaching and believing it.

"Finally they arrested Mr. Yakub. But, it only increased the teachings. They kept persecuting and arresting Yakub's followers until they filled all the jails.

"The officers finally reported to the King that there was no room to put a prisoner in -- if arrested. All the jails are filled; and, when we go out into the streets, we find them still teaching. What shall we do with them? The King questioned the officers on just what the teachings were; and of the name of the leader.

"The officers gave the King the answers to everything. The King said: This is not the name of that man. On entering the prison, the King was shown Yakub's cell. Wa-Alaikum. The King said: So you are Mr. Yakub? He said: Yes, I am. The King said: Yakub, I have come to see if we could work out some agreement that would bring about an end to this trouble. What would you suggest?

"Mr. Yakub told the King: If you give me and my followers everything to start civilization as you have, and furnish us with money and other necessities of life for twenty years, I will take my followers and we will go from you.

"The King was pleased with the suggestion or condition made by Yakub, and agreed to take care of them for twenty years, until Yakub's followers were able to go for themselves.

"After learning who Mr. Yakub was, they all were afraid of him, and were glad to make almost any agreement with him and his followers.

"This history or future of Mr. Yakub and his people was in the Nation's Book, by the writers (23 Scientists) of our history, 8,400 years before his birth. So, the Government began to make preparation for the exiling of Mr. Yakub and his followers. The King ordered everyone rounded up who was a believer in Mr. Yakub. They took them to the seaport and loaded them on ships.

"After rounding them all up into ships, they numbered 59,999. Yakub made 60,000. Their ships sailed out to an Isle in the Aegean Sea called Pelan (Bible Patmos). After they were loaded into the ships, Mr. Yakub examined each of them to see if they were 100 per cent with him; and to see if they were all healthy and productive people. If not, he would throw them off. Some were found to be unfit and overboard they went...

"Mr. Yakub's charge to his laborers was very strict -- death if one disobeyed. They didn't know what Yakub had in mind until they were given their labor to do. He made his laborers, from the chief to the least, liars. The doctor lied about the blood of the two black people who wanted to marry, that it did not mix...

Here we see why Jesus of 2000 years ago was made to say, "You belong to your father, the devil, and you want to carry out your father's desires. He was a murderer from the beginning, not holding to the truth, for there is no truth in him. When he lies, he speaks his native language, for he is a liar and the father of lies...." *(John 8:44)*

Mr. Yakub was a scientist or god. The vile world government structure we live under today is rooted in his literature or writings prepared 6,600 years ago and some of what Moses (Musa) taught to Yakub's people 4,000 years ago parts they had forgotten.

He understood the genetic nature the self and original black nation. The word "gene" is often used to refer to the hereditary *cause* of a human trait. In genetics, these traits are either **PP—black dominant**, **Bp—brown, red, yellow incomplete dominance** or **aa—pale recessive**. Hence, his man was made based upon the number six (6 variations of gene combinations), through the act of sex or breeding the incomplete dominance into its final recessive trait. **See Genotype Map on pg. 29.**

When this was accomplished, the recessive race was calloused together as graft to depend upon the root of civilization's original people's labor. This is now done via government policy, military force and using tricks and lies.

"Of course, Mr. Yakub lived but 150 years; but, his ideas continued in practice. He gave his people guidance in the form of literature. What they should do and how to do it (how to rule the black nation). He said to them: When you become unalike (white), you may return to the Holy Land and people, from whom you were exiled.

"Of course, Mr. Yakub lived but 150 years; but, his ideas continued in practice. He gave his people guidance in the form of literature. What they should do and how to do it (how to rule the black nation). He said to them: When you become unalike (white), you may return to the Holy Land and people, from whom you were exiled.

"The Yakub made devils were really pale white, with really blue eyes; which we think are the ugliest of colors for a human eye. They were called Caucasian -- which means, according to some of the Arab scholars, One whose evil effect is not confined to one's self alone, but affects others.

"There was no good taught to them while on the Island. By teaching the nurses to kill the black baby and save the brown baby, so as to graft the white out of it; by lying to the black mother of the baby, this lie was born into the very nature of the white baby; and, murder for the black people also born in them -- or made by nature a liar and murderer."[14]

Genotype Map

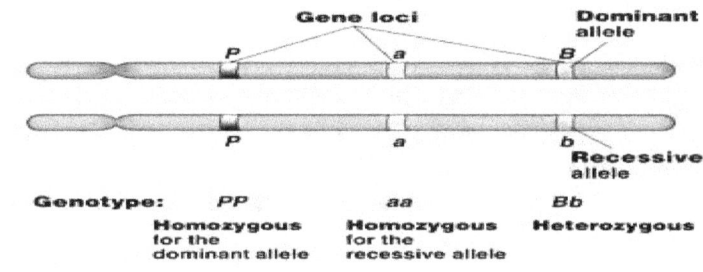

4000 years of Caucasian History

No white scholar or religious scientists knew the details of their missing 2,000 years of their 6,000 year history until the revelation Master W. Fard Muhammad taught to Elijah Muhammad and the Lost and Found members of the Nation of Islam in North America.

According to Jewish scholars and religious scientists, man's history began 4,000 years ago. They propound:

---

[14] Message To The Blackman Chapter 55, "Making of the Devil, by Elijah Muhammad, Messenger of Allah

"We begin counting the Jewish Year One from the creation of Adam who is seen as the physical and spiritual pinnacle in terms of the creation of the world.

"As the Book of Genesis relates it, Adam was created on the sixth day in the process of creation, more than 5760 years ago. (The year 2000 of the Common Era is equivalent to the year 5760 in the Hebrew calendar)

"Adam is unique among the other creatures, inhabiting the earth not just because he gives rise to such an amazingly innovative group of descendants, but because Adam is created *b'tzelem Elohim*, "in the image of God." (Genesis 1:26) This means he has a soul—a *neshama* —a higher, spiritual, intellectual essence. This Divine spark is the God-like essence we human beings all have.

"Once Adam is completed, God then, so to speak, takes off His cosmic watch, hands it to Adam and says, "Now we switch to earth time." A day becomes a revolution of the earth on its axis; a year is the earth going round the sun once, etc. According to Jewish chronology, God took off His watch more than 5760 years ago.

"There is a profound lesson rooted in the idea of starting the Jewish calendar from the completion of Adam. Just as the movie director starts the cameras rolling when the big actors show up on the set (even though years of preparation may have gone into the project before the actual filming starts), so too does God start His earth clock when Adam appears on the planet. The lesson to be learned formed this is that the focus of creation is humanity. God creates an entire universe for human beings. The ultimate question is then, why are we here? What is the purpose of creation?

"Many people believe that God needs us so He created man to serve Him. This is not the Jewish perspective on creation. If God is infinite, then He has no needs or wants. He lacks nothing and there is absolutely nothing we can do for Him. So why were we created?

"One of the most fundamental ideas in Judaism is that God created us give us the ultimate gift: a relationship with Himself, transcendence (in Hebrew the word is *dvekut* - **attachment**). Connecting to God is the ultimate form of relationship and that which our soul ultimately yearns for. Every pleasure we experience and every meaningful relationship we make in this world is just a small taste of the ultimate relationship of our soul with our creator.[15]

As Reverend Al Sharpton always states at the end of his T.V. News Broadcast, *"Nice Try...We Got Chu."*

The missing 2,000 years the dear Jewish Rabbi cannot reveal is what the Honorable Elijah Muhammad revealed from the Word of Master Wallace Fard Muhammad.

---

[15] Rabbi Moshe Chaim Luzzatto, *Derech Hashem I:2:1*

"This is the reason why the American so-called Negroes can never agree on unity among themselves, which would put them on top overnight. The devils keep them divided by paid informers from among themselves. They keep such fools among us. But, the real truth of the devils sometimes converts the informers and brings them over to us as true believers. We don't bother about killing them, as I am not teaching that which I want to be kept as a secret, but that which the world has not known and should know.

"After Yakub's devils were among the Holy people of Islam (the black nation) for six months, they had our people at war with each other. The holy people were unable to understand, just why they could not get along in peace with each other, until they took the matter to the King.

"The King told the holy people of the black nation that the trouble they were having was caused by the white devils in their midst, and that there would be no peace among them until they drove these white made devils from among them.

"The holy people prepared to drive the devils out from among them. The King said: Gather every one of the devils up and strip them of our costume. Put an apron on them to hide their nakedness. Take all literature from them and take them by way of the desert. Send a caravan, armed with rifles, to keep the devils going westward. Don't allow one of them to turn back; and, if they are lucky enough to get across the Arabian

Desert, let them go into the hills of West Asia, the place they now call Europe.

"Yakub's made devils were driven out of Paradise, into the hills of West Asia (Europe), and stripped of everything but the language. They walked across that hot, sandy desert, into the land where long years of both trouble and joy awaited them; but -- they finally made it. (Not all: many died in the desert.)

"Once there, they were roped in, to keep them out of Paradise. To make sure, the Muslims, who lived along the borders of East and West Asia, were ordered to patrol the border to keep Yakub's devils in West Asia (now called Europe), so that the original nation of black man could live in peace; and the devils could be alone to themselves, to do as they pleased, as long as they didn't try crossing the East border.

"The soldiers patrolled the border armed with swords, to prevent the devils from crossing. This went on for 2,000 years. After that time, Musa (Moses) was born: the man whom Allah would send to these exiled devils to bring them again into the light of civilization. Before we take up this first 2,000 years of the devils exiled on our planet, let us not lose sight of what and how they were made, and of the god who made them, Mr. Yakub.

"Just what have we learned, or rather are learning from this divine revelation of our enemies, the devils? Answer: We are learning the truth, which has been kept a secret for 6,000 years concerning the white race, who have deceived us...

"Again, we learn who the Bible (Genesis 1:16) is referring to in the saying: Let us make man. This US was fifty-nine thousand, nine hundred and ninety-nine (59,999) black men and women; making or grafting them into the likeness or image of the original man...

"...After 2,000 years of living as a savage, Allah raised up Musa (Moses) to bring the white race again into civilization: to take their place as rulers, as Yakub has intended for them. Musa (Moses) became their God and leader. He brought them out of the caves; taught them to believe in Allah; taught them to wear clothes; how to cook their food; how to season it with salt; what beef they should kill and eat; and, how to use fire for their service. Moses taught them against putting the female cow under burden.[16]

*19. When we resurrected them, they asked each other, 'How long have you been here?' 'We have been here one day or part of the day,' they answered. 'Your Lord knows best how long we stayed here, so let us send one of us with this money to the city. Let him fetch the cleanest food, and buy some for us. Let him **keep a low profile, and attract no attention.** 20. 'If they discover you, they will stone you, or force you to revert to their*

---

[16] Message To The Blackman Chapter 55, "Making of the Devil, by Elijah Muhammad, Messenger of Allah

religion, then you can never succeed.' 21. We caused them to be discovered, to let everyone know that GOD's promise is true, and to remove all doubt concerning the end of the world..." (Holy Quran 18:15; 19-21)

Let me stop her and say, the Old Testament book of Leviticus was given to the Jews by Moses. In fact, he provided what is called the first five books of the Old Testament to help them carry out what Yakub had promised 2,000 years earlier. What Moses taught aided Caucasians to eventually come among the original black people of the holy land, **by keeping a low profile**, to carry out the remaining 4,000 years of their rule.

Since the Caucasians rule over the original black nations of the earth, of the 5 billion original people, by the time of the coming of Master Fard Muhammad, in 1934, only 4.6 billion originals survived the war, bloodshed and mischief making of Yakub's grafted race.

Of course, Mr. Yakub repented that he ever made (devil) as stated in Genesis 6:6, *"And it repented the Lord that he made man (devil) on Earth and it grieved him at heart."* As you can see the man Yakub is also hidden under the title Lord too.[17]

---

[17] The Final Call to Islam Published by Elijah Muhammad August 25, 1934 Article by Lonnie Pasha

Chapter Four

What is Grafting

Revelation means a surprising and previously unknown fact, especially one made in a dramatic way. It is the making known of a secret or the unknown—apocalypse.

"In the book of Revelation the Tribe of Joseph represents the other children of Joseph after Manasseh and Ephraim. Manasseh was made equivalent to a son of **Jacob/Israel (Supplanter)** by Jacob himself at the end of the Book of Genesis. In the Book of Ezekiel, God **grafted** the Tribe of Ephraim to the Tribe of Judah, so in the Book of Revelation, The Tribe of Ephraim is represented by the Tribe of Judah by **graft**..."[18]

I hope you over stand the above wisdom and its meaning...who stole your soul black man and women? Answer: The same people who stole our forefathers from West Africa.

In the science of grafting, that which is being grafted must depend upon the root of the thing it is attached too. For example, the graft (scion) and the rootstock are calloused (or knitted) together. All suckers [root knowledge] are removed from the

---

[18] http://en.wikipedia.org/wiki/Ephraim

rootstock; then the scion [implant] is allowed to grow, thus maintaining its true identity.[19]

So while the white race or people were genetically and physically made from the 6 genotypes contained within the original black nation, they have economically, grafted-in or depend upon the original black or dark nations of the earth for resources to remain in power and control. In addition, to assure a successful grafting process, the original ancient knowledge is removed from the mind of the original nation. Otherwise, Yakub's made-grafted race would not have known their true identity.

This idea of grafting might be over stood better in horticulture grafting. To grasp this concept, grafting is a life cell technique whereby tissues from one plant are inserted into those of another so that the two sets of vascular tissues *(cell tissues transporting fluid and nutrients internally)* are calloused together as two different genus (kin).[20]

"He Mr. Yakub – the mighty scientist and maker of the white race or white man was no fool by no means, just because he made an enemy for us. This made us still great to know that in us was the germ of a whole race of people – that we could form him and teach him then make him rule the teacher, for a certain length of time,

---

[19] http://www.starkbros.com/blog/science-of-grafting/
[20] The term comes from the Latin genus meaning "descent, family, type, gender", cognate with Greek: γένος – genos, "race, stock, kin"

until the people produce on greater than he (Yacub)...Now, today..."A Saviour is born"... out of the germ, out of the plunder..."He's made partly from the race of Yacub and partly from His own, just for the purpose to save you and me..."[21]

Being recessive is not what made the white race practice so much evil throughout the ages of their history; of course, it did make them concupiscent *(a desire of the lower appetite contrary to reason)* by nature. What has enabled them to exercise such vile ruling powers was/is the literature they were taught from the beginning, while on Patmos Isles, by their father, Yakub.

Grafting is not done by nature, but is unnaturally a man-made process. This is why the biblical words of Genesis ask the question *"Lets us make man..."* This question was not posed by Allah (God) the Creator of Self and the Universe because He did not ask permission from any one to create trillions of years ago. The words articulated in Genesis represent what Mr. Yakub propositioned to his followers 6,600 years ago. Then after they had all agreed with him, he proceeded with his scientific made-man grafting experimentation. The result, after 600 years, is the white race. In the begging, this people were the first blue eyed, blond haired, pale skin 100% recessive

---

[21] www.muhammadspeaks.com/news.html

men and women. Once more, it took 600 years to degrade black (eumelanin) into its weakest most lethal recessive trait (wrinkle) that was "kin" to our life cell's 6 genotypes.

"Melanin comes in two types: phaeomelanin (red to yellow) and eumelanin (dark brown to black)."[22]

Those with 100% recessive (aa) traits represent the new race of people Yakub grafted 6,600 years ago on Isles Patmos.

What is being made known here is how science categorizes all people into a haplogroup. In the study of molecular evolution, a haplogroup represents the relationship each ethnic group has with a common ancestor—Ancient Asiatic black nation. In hindsight, with respect to the genetic nature of white or pale skin people, they are indicative of the recessive gene (aa). Black skin is indicative of the dominant gene (PP); and Brown, Red and Yellow are indicative of the incomplete dominant gene (Ba).

Today no intelligent person argues over the fact that all people derive from Black skin man and woman of the earth. In human genetics, **Haplogroup A** (M91) is a Y-chromosome haplogroup. Haplogroup A is found mainly in the Southern Nile region and Southern Africa. It represents the oldest and most diverse of the human

---

[22] http://en.wikipedia.org/wiki/Melanin

Y-chromosome haplogroups. It is believed to be the haplogroup corresponding to Y-chromosomal Adam.[23]

"The book of Jewish traditions called the Midrash Rabbah actually uses [a] Bible story to explain the birth of White children to Black parents. The rabbis present this parable:

> *The king of the Arabs put this question to Rabbi Akiba: "I am Black and my wife is Black, yet she gave birth to a White son. Shall I kill her for having played the harlot while lying with me?" Said the other, "Are the figures in your house painted Black or White?" "White," he said. The other assured him, "When you had intercourse with her, she fixed her eyes upon the White figures and bore a child like them."[24]*

Since the leaders of the white race did not fully recognize or know their first 2,000 years on earth, they now work very hard to hide the truth about their origin using lies and fairytales. Not so with the revelation taught by the Honorable Elijah Muhammad. He said:

"...Now that they are the same, but have the ways of a human being they are referred to as mankind -- not the real original man, but a being made like the original in the sense of human beings.

---

[23] http://en.wikipedia.org/wiki/Haplogroup
[24] http://www.finalcall.com/artman/publish/Perspectives_1/article_7371.shtml

"The Holy Quran throws a great light on the truth of the creation of this pale, white race of devils. O mankind, surely we have created you from a male and a female (Holy Quran 49:15). This makes it very easy to understand to whom it is referring. What mankind? Surely we created man from sperm mixed (with ovum) to try him, so we have made him hearing and seeing (Holy Quran 76:2).

"Inasmuch as these chapters have a further reference to the spiritual creation of the Last Messenger, it is equally true that they refer to the physical creation of the white race. In another place, the Holy Quran says: "'We have created man, and now he is an open disputer.'"[25]

In Brief, the spiritual making of the Last Messenger in based upon the concept of Immaculate Conception wherein the **Word of God** was used to impregnate him with truth. This truth in turn is to produce a new nation or civilization out of the pillage of Yakub's civilization. But before this new nation comes to full power and authority, they would be attacked to prevent from getting right up to the door of life in the hereafter; after being in servitude for more than 430 years in North America. Fact is, the 2nd book of Revelation take us up to imaginations of the hereafter (heaven on earth) but not into the actual life itself. This knowledge is now with the Last Messenger who awaits to bring it about through his servant and representative [Revelations 10]. More on Last Messenger in chapter 5.

---

[25] Message To The Blackman Chapter 55, "Making of the Devil, by Elijah Muhammad, Messenger of Allah

Chapter Five

John the Revelator is Yakub

For many years, Patmos was a place of pilgrimage for Catholics and Orthodox, since it is where Saint John the Divine wrote the Book of Revelation (the Apocalypse).[26] According to the Christian story, John was banished to Patmos under the Roman rule of Domitian, but not so fast. Truth is according to the Honorable Elijah Muhammad, Yakub and 60,000 of his followers were banished to Patmos over 6,600 years ago for rebellion against the righteous rulers of the holy land.

"Since we have learned that Mr. Yakub was an original man (black) the ignorant of our people may say: If Yakub was a black man and the father of the devils, then he was a devil. That is like one saying the horse is as much a mule as the mule.

"Or, that an orange or lemon is as much grapefruit as the grapefruit: because the grapefruit is grafted from the orange and lemon. They are not alike because the grafted is no longer original."

The Honorable Elijah Muhammad and Minister Louis Farrakhan have revealed the truth about John the

---

[26] http://en.wikipedia.org/wiki/John_of_Patmos

Revelator (**John of Patmos**).[27] This particular man is actually Yakub. Being the father of the idea into how to graft a new people from the sperm cell of the original black nation, Yakub foresaw the beginning and ending of his made race and their vile society. The warning book (Bible Revelations) he wrote now contains 403 verses and 22 chapters describing the end of the Caucasians rule over the nations of the earth. It also gives us a glimpse at the door of the Hereafter— Heaven on Earth while we live; which opens up after The Final War. This final conclusion of Yakub's (Jacob/Israel/Caucasian race) vile world order, he saw in a vision while one the Isles of Patmos (Pelan) in the Aegean Sea in year 9,000 scheduled on the Asiatic calendar [Revelation 1:9]. Although he saw and wrote about future events, the most important warning was about the commercial fall of his civilization and the birth of a New Divine Supreme Being, His Last Messenger and a new way of life (civilization) to come on earth.

Yakub's major prophecies were about events that would occur during the 18th, 19th, 20th, and 21st century i.e., end-times! Yakub captured these events in the 17th 18[th,] 19th, and 20th book of his warning book (Revelation).

---

[27] The Final Call to Islam Published by Elijah Muhammad August 25, 1934 Article by Lonnie Pasha

With an open mind, we must take these books to represent what occurred to Great Britain's empire after 1870 up to 1914 (end of their Gold Standard), to the birth of Master Fard Muhammad in 1877 (God in Person), and to the meeting between Elijah Muhammad and Master **FARD** Muhammad (September 1931). One more observation regarding these end-times is the grave set of circumstances unfolding in the wilderness of North America—her trillion trillions of commercial paper money debt from 2013 until her fall. So let see...

In Revelations 17, Yakub was taken by the spirit of God's angel to see into the future work of his grafted or made-race. The symbolism used to describe what he saw was added centuries later by the wicked translators. Nevertheless, what he wrote is being fulfilled in the wilderness of North America's in terms of her political and foreign policy, the condition of the once holy black people held as a lawful captive, the work of God's last Messenger, his followers and their detractors. Lastly, he was made to see why a New God will execute Judgment not on a city, but an entire civilization established by YAKUB'S grafted race in 1776

[Revelations 17:1-18] *¹One of the seven angels who had the seven bowls came and said to me, "Come, I will show you the punishment of the great prostitute, who sits by many waters. ²With her the kings of the earth committed adultery and the inhabitants of the earth were intoxicated with the wine of her adulteries."³ Then the angel carried me away in the Spirit into a wilderness. There I saw a woman sitting on a scarlet beast that was covered with blasphemous names and had seven heads and ten horns. ⁴ The woman was dressed in purple and*

scarlet, and was glittering with gold, precious stones and pearls. She held a golden cup in her hand, filled with abominable things and the filth of her adulteries. ⁵ The name written on her forehead was a mystery:

BABYLON THE GREAT
THE MOTHER OF PROSTITUTES
AND OF THE ABOMINATIONS OF THE EARTH.

Statue of Liberty

⁶ I saw that the woman was drunk with the blood of God's holy people, the blood of those who bore testimony to Jesus. When I saw her, I was greatly astonished. ⁷ Then the angel said to me: "Why are you astonished? I will explain to you the mystery of the woman and of the beast she rides, which has the seven heads and ten horns. ⁸ The beast, which you saw, once was, now is not, and yet will come up out of the Abyss and go to its destruction. The inhabitants of the earth whose names have not been written in the book of life from the creation of the world will be astonished when they see the beast, because it once was, now is not, and yet will come.

⁹ "This calls for a mind with wisdom. The seven heads are seven hills on which the woman sits. ¹⁰ They are also seven kings. Five have fallen, one is, the other has not yet come; but when he does come, he must remain for only a little while. [11] The beast who once was, and now is not, is an eighth king. He belongs to the seven and is going to his destruction.

[12] *"The ten horns you saw are ten kings who have not yet received a kingdom, but who for one hour will receive authority as kings along with the beast. [13] They have one purpose and will give their power and authority to the beast. [14] They will wage war against the Lamb **[Last Message of God]**, but the Lamb will triumph over them because he is Lord of lords and King of kings—and with him will be his called, chosen and faithful followers."*

[15] *Then the angel said to me, "The waters you saw, where the prostitute sits, are peoples, multitudes, nations and languages. [16] The beast and the ten horns you saw will hate the prostitute. They will bring her to ruin and leave her naked; they will eat her flesh and burn her with fire. [17] For God has put it into their hearts to accomplish his purpose by agreeing to hand over to the beast their royal authority, until God's words are fulfilled. [18] The woman you saw is the great city that rules over the kings of the earth."*

In verses 16 to 18, Yakub symbolically expose how the United States—a Federal Corporation[28] will ultimately loose its vassal governments that once supported her policies, treasury bonds and commercial paper money.

---

[28] **28 USC § 3002** – Legal Definition of United States

To conclude this segment, is it coincidence that around the head of the Statue of Liberty is seven points. Is it a coincidence how this lady is surrounded by water on Ellis Island? Is this what Yakub foresaw on Patmos 6,600 years ago--America?

> *(Revelations 17:9)* *"This calls for a mind with wisdom. The seven heads are seven hills on which the woman sits."*

> *(Revelations 17:15)* *"Then the angel said to me, "The waters you saw, where the prostitute sits, are peoples, multitudes, nations and languages."*

In Revelations 18, Yakub also describes how the other nations of earth will see and hear about Great Brittan's daughter—America, the mystery Babylon's fall and how all other commercial governments will be ill-affected. These other governments; of course, have shared in the United States—a Federal Corporation's pleasure, and gained by her wealth and trade; therefore, they mourned to see her economic fall.

[Revelations 18:4-19] *"4Then I heard another voice from heaven say:"'Come out of her, my people,' so that you will not share in her sins, so that you will not receive any of her plagues; 5for her sins are piled up to heaven, and God has remembered her crimes. 6 Give back to her as she has given; pay her back double for what she has done. Pour her a double portion from her own cup. 7 Give her as much torment and grief as the glory and luxury she gave herself. In her heart she boasts, 'I sit enthroned as queen. I am not a widow; I will never mourn.'* ⁸ *Therefore in one day her plagues will overtake her: death, mourning and famine. She will be consumed by fire, for mighty is the Lord God who judges her.* ⁹ *"When the kings of the earth who committed adultery with her and shared her luxury see the smoke of her burning, they will weep and mourn over her.* ¹⁰ *Terrified at her torment, they will stand far off and cry:*

> "'**Woe! Woe to you, great city,**
> **you mighty city of Babylon!**
> **In one hour your doom has come!**'

¹¹ *"The merchants of the earth will weep and mourn over her because no one buys their cargoes anymore—* ¹² *cargoes of gold, silver, precious stones and pearls; fine linen, purple, silk and scarlet cloth; every sort of citron wood, and articles of every kind made of ivory, costly wood, bronze, iron and marble;* ¹³ *cargoes of cinnamon and spice, of incense, myrrh and frankincense, of wine and olive oil, of fine flour and wheat; cattle and sheep; horses and carriages; and human beings sold as slaves.*

¹⁴ *"They will say, 'The fruit you longed for is gone from you. All your luxury and splendor have vanished, never to be recovered.'* ¹⁵ *The merchants who sold these things and gained their wealth from her will stand far off, terrified at her torment. They will weep and mourn* ¹⁶ *and cry out:*

> '**Woe! Woe to you, great city,**
> **dressed in fine linen, purple and scarlet,**
> **and glittering with gold, precious stones and pearls!**'

17 In one hour such great wealth has been brought to ruin!' "Every sea captain, and all who travel by ship, the sailors, and all who earn their living from the sea, will stand far off. 18 When they see the smoke of her burning, they will exclaim, 'Was there ever a city like this great city?' 19 They will throw dust on their heads, and with weeping and mourning cry out:

Christian scholars have attempted to interpret the above by writings. Some uphold the following:

"The kings of the earth, whom she flattered into idolatry, allowing them to be tyrannical over their subjects, while obedient to her; and the merchants, those who trafficked for her indulgences, pardons, and honours; these mourn. Babylon's friends partook her sinful pleasures and profits, but are not willing to share her plagues...

"...The fall of Babylon was an act of God's justice. And because it was a final ruin, this enemy should never molest them anymore; of this they were assured by a sign."[29]

In Revelations 19, Yakub envisioned and wrote about the God he called Faithful and True with All Power to make war with the vile world his grafted race were made to rule.

---

[29] http://www.christnotes.org/commentary.php?com=mhc&b=66&c=18

[Revelation 19:11-16]. [11] And I saw heaven opened, and behold a white horse; and he that sat upon him was called Faithful and True, and in righteousness he doth judge and make war. *"[12] His eyes were as a flame of fire, and on his head were many crowns; and **he had a name written, that no man knew, but he himself..."*** Obviously, Yakub could not envision His name therefore he wrote, *"**he had a name written, that no man knew, but he himself.**"* Well we now know His name is Wallace Fard Muhammad, the Great Mahdi of the Muslims and Messiah of the Christians. Other prophets also described His coming in Hebrew 10:5 by saying, *"Sacrifice and offering Thou has not desired, but a body Thou hast prepared for Me."* Who is this Person? He is the Supreme Being coming out of hiding. When Elijah met Him face to face, not in 1913, but 1931, He gave the meaning of His name **FARD** (One whom all are obligated to submit). Of course, this aligns with Revelations 19:13.

Christian scholars say Revelations 19 verse 13 mean His name is "**The Word of God**;" a name none fully knows but himself; only this we know, that this Word was God manifest in the flesh; but his perfections cannot be fully understood by any creature.[30] Well in this, we have it! The very *Word of God* means: All is obligated to submit. *"And he was clothed with vesture dipped in blood: and his name is called The Word of God."* (Revelations 19:13)

[14] And the armies which were in heaven followed him upon white horses, clothed in fine linen, white and clean.

---

[30] http://www.christnotes.org/commentary.php?com=mhc&b=66&c=19

15 And out of his mouth goeth a sharp sword, that with it he should smite the nations: and he shall rule them with a rod of iron: and he treadeth the winepress of the fierceness and wrath of Almighty God. 16 And he hath on his vesture and on his thigh a name written, KING OF KINGS, AND LORD OF LORDS. "

War Against Islam

The war against Islam now taking place by Yakub's civilization, is it not against Islam as such, it is against the God of Islam, all His forces of nature and His angels.

In fact, Yakub also envisioned and wrote about one of the seven Islamic angels assigned to use the sun as a weapon of war during these end-times

[Revelations 19:17-21]. *17 And I saw an angel standing in the sun; and he cried with a loud voice, saying to all the fowls that fly in the midst of heaven, Come and gather yourselves together unto the supper of the great God; 18 That ye may eat the flesh of kings, and the flesh of captains, and the flesh of mighty men, and the flesh of horses, and of them that sit on them, and the flesh of all men, both free and bond, both small and great. 19 And I saw the beast, and the kings of the earth, and their armies, gathered together to make war against him that sat on the horse, and against his army. 20 And the beast was taken, and with him the false prophet that wrought miracles before him, with which he deceived them that had received the mark of the beast, and them that worshipped his image. These both were cast alive into a lake of fire burning with brimstone.[21] And the remnant were slain with the sword of him that sat upon the horse, which sword proceeded out of his mouth: and all the fowls were filled with their flesh."*

Besides extreme heat waves, the sun will be used to run interference with the communication systems. Make no mistake about it. Yakub knew the angels of Allah are highly trained righteous men with super consciousness, unlike the men of war of Yakub's civilization who have displayed the worst form of lying, drinking, gambling, raping, lynching, burning, stealing, robbing, disrespect of person and persons. Who have displayed the worst form of nail painting, face painting, swine eating, public nudity and colonies, nudie newspapers and magazines, nude church-goers, and profane language users in the name of democracy and freedom!

The angels of Allah have the consciousness to use the forces of rain, hail, snow and earth quakes to fulfill what has been written of them throughout the book of Revelations. According to the writings of Yakub's vision on Patmos, these events will be fulfilled and ended by the 21th century. What shall exist in 2022? But I digress.

The way some Christian scholars interpret Revelations 19 is as follows:

"Angels and saints follow, and are like Christ in their armour of purity and righteousness. The threatenings of the written word he is going to execute on his enemies. The ensigns of his authority are his name; asserting his authority and power, warning the most powerful princes to submit or they must fall before him. The powers of earth and hell make their utmost effort. These verses declare important events, foretold by the prophets. These persons were not excused because they did what their leaders bade them. How vain will be the plea of many sinners at the great day! We followed our guides; we did as we saw others do! God has given a rule to walk by, in his word; neither the example of the most, nor of the chief, must influence us contrary thereto: if we do as the most do, we must go where the most go, even into the burning lake."[31]

The Honorable Minister Louis Farrakhan elaborated upon the meaning of the phrase "Lake of Fire." He said:

"The Honorable Elijah Muhammad said that Master Fard Muhammad, the Man Who Saviours' Day in the Nation of Islam honors, studied 42 years to deliver us. We were never told all that He studied, but in order to deliver us from the powerful hands of those who oppress us, He first had to study The Enemy that would work to prevent us from being taken...

"...This man, *Master Fard Muhammad*, Elijah Muhammad said of Him that He came to us from the Holy City of Mecca, in Arabia. He was born February

---

[31] http://www.christnotes.org/commentary.php?com=mhc&b=66&c=19

26, 1877. He knew His future when He was six years old: He saw himself pushing the DuPonts, the Rockefellers, and the House of Rothschild—this Synagogue of Satan—into a Lake of Fire when He matured.

"Master Fard Muhammad was made from Black and White so that He could slip in among us undetected, as the Bible teaches "He would come as a thief in the night." The Honorable Elijah Muhammad said of this Man that He is a world traveler Who had visited every inhabited part of our planet. He spoke 16 different languages, and wrote 10. He extracted the language, and pictured the people on Mars. He told us of life on all of the planets. He spoke the language of the birds.

"It was Master Fard Muhammad Who pointed out to us a dreadful-looking Plane in the sky, a half-a-mile by a half-a-mile. A Plane that had Two Natures and Two Functions like Himself: He is a Saviour, but He also is a Destroyer! And that Wheel that is above our head has those same Two Functions. One to heal, one to save; one to replenish, one to renew the Earth and the people on it! But another that is to destroy The Enemy of Peace, so that those who live on our planet after such destruction will never again have to worry about a mischief maker or peace breaker, breaking the Peace of the members of the Human Family![32]

This teaching also aligns with what Mr. Yakub envisioned on the Isles of Patmos (Pelan); particularly, about a mechanical city in the sky.

In Revelations 21, Yakub saw a new righteous government establishment replacing his old wicked government establishment. The new government, he realized, will model the blueprint of the life and science lived on a mechanical city in the sky designed by God Himself. Yakub referred to this city as a New Jerusalem—the place where God and His angels will launch war against Satan's army. Then after the great battle and victory, a new  civilization will be taught and established throughout the ends of the earth forever through the Resurrection of the once lost Black Nation and not Yakub's world order.

The question is: Is New Jerusalem also referred to as the Mother Plane? Unlike the U.S. and Russian space station, the Mother Plane was designed by Master Fard Muhammad. **See Image of U.S. Space Station above.** Compared to the mechanical city seen below, the U.S. and Russian Space Station above is a child-like contraption. I mean Western astrophysicists of aero-space dynamics are millions of years behind in applying the mechanical sciences of the universe to employ in a battle in the sky against God (Allah) and His angels.

PHOTOGRAPHED BY HUBBLE TELESCOPE
February 8, 1994

According to Weekly World News...Just days after space shuttle astronauts repaired the Hubble Space Telescope in mid December, the giant lens focused on a star cluster at the edge of the universe... That's the word from author and researcher Marcia Masson, who quoted highly, places NASA insiders as having said that the telescope beamed hundreds of photos back to the command center at Goddard Space Flight Center in Greenbelt, Md., on December 26.

'The pictures clearly show a vast white city floating eerily in the blackness of space.'

And the expert quoted NASA sources as saying that the city is definitely Heaven "because life as we know it couldn't possibly exist in icy, airless space. "This is it – this is the proof we've been waiting for," Dr. Masson told reporters. "Through an enormous stroke of luck, NASA aimed the Hubble Telescope at precisely the right place at precisely the right time to capture these images on film. I'm not particularly religious, but I don't doubt that somebody or something influenced the decision to aim the telescope at that particular area of space. "Was that someone or something God himself? Given the vastness of the universe, and all the places NASA could have targeted for study that would certainly appear to be the case."

NASA spokesmen declined to comment on the author's report "pending further analysis of the photographs received on December 26." In spite of official silence, agency insiders concede that NASA "has discovered something that might alter the future of all mankind."

They also confirmed that President Bill Clinton and Vice President Al Gore have taken a keen personal interest in the photographs and have requested daily briefings. Dr. Masson said: "The Hubble Space Telescope was designed to photograph images as far away as the edge of the universe but a lens flaw prevented it from doing so until shuttle astronauts corrected the defect during a recent mission.[33]

Yakub seems to have described the future work of a holy city in the sky as best he could while on Patmos. He at least knew this holy city contained an entirely new atmosphere without any opposite polarities *(a relation between two opposite attributes or tendencies)*. He knew one day [**REV. 22:1-5**] that the negative earth would be perfected by the powers on the holy city. Not by the U.S. Space Station and the experiments they hope to achieve to affect our earth's atmosphere and human life.

---

[33] http://weeklyworldnews.com/headlines/11684/new-hubble-images/

[Revelation 21:1]. "*1 Now I saw a new heaven and a new earth, for the first heaven and the first earth had passed away. Also there was no more sea. 2 Then I, John, saw the holy city, New Jerusalem, coming down out of heaven from God, prepared as a bride adorned for her husband. 3 And I heard a loud voice from heaven saying, "Behold, the tabernacle of God is with men, and He will dwell with them, and they shall be His people. God Himself will be with them and be their God. 4 And God will wipe away every tear from their eyes; there shall be no more death, nor sorrow, nor crying. There shall be no more pain, for the former things have passed away." 5 Then He who sat on the throne said, "Behold, I make all things new." And He said to me, "Write, for these words are true and faithful." 6 And He said to me, "It is done! I am the Alpha and the Omega, the Beginning and the End. I will give of the fountain of the water of life freely to him who thirsts. 7 He who overcomes shall inherit all things, and I will be his God and he shall be My son. 8 But the cowardly, unbelieving, abominable, murderers, sexually immoral, sorcerers, idolaters, and all liars shall have their part in the lake which burns with fire and brimstone, which is the second death." 9 Then one of the seven angels who had the seven bowls filled with the seven last plagues came to me and talked with me, saying, "Come, I will show you the bride, the Lamb's wife."*

The symbolic meaning of the word Lamb represents the Last Messenger of God who escapes death and his bride represents those who accept the truth revealed to him by (Allah) God in the Personage of Master Wallace **Fard** Muhammad.

On December 22, 1967 the Honorable Elijah Muhammad wrote in the Muhammad Speaks Newspaper and said this about Yakub's civilization mentioned in Revelation:

"...EVIL could not capture us 100 per cent, within 6,000 years, due to the Mahdi (Messiah) being born at the end of 6,000 years from the birth of Yakub (the father of the white race), whose wisdom was limited to the birth and coming of the Great Mahdi, God in Person, (of the righteous).

"The coming of the Mahdi as being One greater in knowledge and greater in wisdom than Yakub was seen and prophesied by Yakub and he prophesied His coming after him to destroy his civilization in Revelation.

"IT IS mentioned that he saw One coming after him Whose brightness (wisdom) of His coming would destroy his made man and his made man's wisdom (the white race), for it is superior wisdom that rules the people.

"The world of the white race is angry because of the superior wisdom of the Mahdi that is being taught to the inferior – especially the America so-called Negroes. It is angering them and finally will cause a complete vanishing of the wisdom of the white race which has rule Black people like a savage beast and which now tries to deceive those who are yet asleep to the knowledge of the white race by showing false friendship, false promises of wealth, and high positions in his government.

"BEING ignorant of such teachings coming from the slave master's children will cause the destruction of hundreds of thousands and maybe millions of so-called American Negroes seeking temporary enjoyment of life from their enemies.

"They will get all of this permanently from the Great Mahdi (Master Fard Muhammad) who will fulfill His promise to us if we believe. He promised heaven at once to the Negro believers."

How did Yakub envision the holy city in Revelation 21? Continue to read what he wrote while on Patmos 6,600 years ago.

10 And he carried me away in the Spirit to a great and high mountain, and showed me the great city, the holy Jerusalem, descending out of heaven from God, 11 having the glory of God. Her light was like a most precious stone, like a jasper stone, clear as crystal. 12 Also she had a great and high wall with twelve gates, and twelve angels at the gates, and names written on them, which are the names of the twelve tribes of the children of Israel: 13 three gates on the east, three gates on the north, three gates on the south, and three gates on the west. 14 Now the wall of the city had twelve foundations, and on them were the names of the twelve apostles of the Lamb. 15 And he who talked with me had a gold reed to measure the city, its gates, and its wall. 16 The city is laid out as a square; its length is as great as its breadth. And he measured the city with the reed: twelve thousand furlongs. Its length, breadth, and height are equal. 17 Then he measured its wall: one hundred and forty-four cubits, according to the measure of a man, that is, of an angel. [18] The construction of its wall was of jasper; and the city was pure gold, like clear glass. [19] The foundations of the wall of the city were adorned with all kinds of precious stones: the first foundation was jasper, the second sapphire, the third chalcedony, the fourth emerald, [20] the fifth sardonyx, the sixth sardius, the seventh chrysolite, the eighth beryl, the ninth topaz, the tenth chrysoprase, the eleventh jacinth, and the twelfth amethyst. [21] The twelve gates were twelve pearls: each individual gate was of one pearl. And the street of the city was pure gold, like transparent glass.

So far, from his description, this mechanical object in the sky or Mother Plane consists of all earthly materials and its inhabitants represent undefiled members of the original Asiatic black nation who took flight with it. According to the teachings of the Honorable Elijah Muhammad, the Mother Plane went up in 1929 and it took 20 years to complete. **FARD** Muhammad began construction of this marvelous Ship in 1910 during the era when all European commercial governments used the Gold Standard. The cost to produce its material was $150 million in Gold. Yes she was made on this earth under the direct command and science of God Himself to destroy Yakub's civilization from the sky. And yes, this God is the New God whom Jewish Rabbi's might say has the secrets of the *merkabah (*all the secrets of creation)."

Master **FARD** Muhammad is the Holy One promising members of the Lost and Found Black Nation of Islam to be taught the mechanics of the universe and square off the nations of our earth. Why, because the earth is our turf. Her diameter is 7,926 miles, her circumference is 24,896 miles, her volume is 1,097,509,500,000,000,000,000 sextillion cubic meters and her weight is 6,000,000,000,000,000,000,000 sextillion tons! She floats through space at 18.5 miles per second, moving 4°(degrees) every 15 minutes spinning on her axis at 1,037.3 miles per hour. To complete a 360° circumambulation around the sun in one-solar year; in total, her journey is 584,000,000 million miles. If one can imagine, the high mathematical science of the mechanics applied in making the Mother Plane from earth, you would be God in Person.

After Yakub's visionary description of the Mother Plane was given to his people, Prophet Ezekiel [Ezekiel 10:1] gave his version of it several thousand years after Yakub. But no one has ever described it so clear and concise as Master Fard Muhammad (Allah, God in Person) revealed its purpose and function to the Last Messenger, Honorable Elijah Muhammad—the Lamb of God or exalted Christ. [Revelations 4 and 5]

The following statement, regarding the Mother Plane, was made by the Honorable Elijah Muhammad:

"It is dangerous to declare war and opposition against God (Allah). It is foolish to think that you have the power and the skill to block God's Plan; it is foolish. Today, America's Government is trying to absolutely hide the knowledge of what she sees and what she hears of the truth. As God (Allah) has said to me, and I have taught it to you, that there is a plane in the sky above America, made like a wheel, which is the fulfillment of the prophecy of Ezekiel 10th Chapter, 1st Verse; that he saw it in a vision, that it rose up from the Earth so high that it looked dreadful, and that there was nothing above it except the starry canopy.

"Today, that Plane is in the air and the scientists and the astronomers of America, have seen it here. Mr. Khowule, an ex-General of the United States Armed Forces of America, bears me witness that it is up there, and have dotted around America's planes in the sky, her in America...

" Today, you would like to dismiss it as a lie, but those who peep through the glass (the telescope) and see this plane, do not consider it a lie....An absolute Man-Made-Planet, moving at such terrific speed that you could hardly imagine it; flickers amid the stars of Heaven. Out of the reaches of your (the Devil's) fire, you can't reach it, you can't shoot it down; it's impossible! You can't go to it, you can't capture it; it's impossible! I say, my listeners, "Know that the doom, the Judgment approaches. Know that it is time to repent."

SUPREME WISDOM DEPARTMENT
(OUR MOTHER PLANE)

1. The Mother Plane is made of the finest steel in Asia.

2. It was made on the Island of Nippon (Japan) in 1929, and also took flight that same year.

3. Black, Brown, Red and Yellow Scientists built the Mother Plane.

4. The Scientists did not know what they were building.

5. Her size is Half-mile by Half-mile square.

6. Her shape is oval.

7. Her speed is up to 9,000 miles per hour.

8. Her flying ability is nine thousand (9,000) miles per hour in any direction, up or down, to or fro, in any direction without making a complete directional turn.

9. Her contents are 1,500 small circular planes, as the devil calls them, "FLYING SAUCERS."

COMMENT: Again, the key words "flying roll" appear which is an adequate description for the scout ships

Cuba, Island of Cayolargo del Sur - January 7, 2013, 18:27 local time

(Circular Planes) that are aboard the Mother Ship. The ignorant will say that the second verse should be taken on face value. But this is impossible; since the measurements f this "flying roll" is given by the Prophet . . . the length thereof is twenty cubits." (Note: one (1) cubit is an ancient linear measure of about 18 inches, according to the dictionary). Since one (1) cubit is 13 inches, twenty (20) cubits equal 360 inches, or thirty (30) feet, which is the length of this "Flying Roll." ". . . and the breadth thereof is ten (10) cubits;" ends the second verse. Ten cubits equal 180 inches (15) feet which is the width of this "flying roll."

Hence, there is Zachariah, Chapter 5:1-2, we are told of a "Flying Roll" which is THIRTY FEET long and FIFTEEN FEET wide. This is a near perfect description of one of Allah's Circular Planes.

10. These small planes carry three (3) bombs each; they also shoot flames of fire.

11. The Black men who pilot these small planes have been taught from the age of six that they are to do a special job.

12. These pilots can hit any spot in America, blindfolded, as the Devil will soon see.

13. The bombs that the small planes contain weigh two tons each.

14. They are designed to drill into the Earth upon contact, and drill from one (1) to six (6) miles through stone and rock, and to explode, destroying civilization or any living matter (or life) within a fifty (50) mile radius.

15. After these bombs explode, a poisonous gas is found to snuff out the remaining life, if any still exists.

16. The purpose of the Mother Plane is to destroy the wicked place ever to be on the planet Earth at any time (America, the Great Mystery Babylon).

17. Her position is 40 miles out from the Earth's sphere.

18. She holds this position from 6 to 12 months at a time. When this time is up, the Mother Plane comes into the atmosphere to take in fresh air for our Brothers inside, then she retakes her position.

19. At the dropping of the bombs, the flames will reach twelve (12) miles, in all directions.

20. When the destruction comes, America will burn 390 years and take 610 years to cool off. The Great Mystery Babylon (America) will perish in the flames of fire. Allah will even cause the air which we breathe to ignite along with the atmosphere. Every atom will burn in and over America from a height of twelve (12) miles down.

"The country of America will be littered with leaflets from the sky, with readings like this; "You have from eight (8) to ten (10) days to return unto your own. The time of this world is at hand." The leaflets will be written in both English and Arabic, so God (Allah) taught me. After the warning from the sky will follow total destruction by the intense heat of fire.

"And you such people who love America, where lying, drinking, gambling, raping, lynching, burning, stealing, robbing, disrespect of person and persons, nail painting, face painting, swine eating, public nude resorts, nude colonies, nudie newspapers and magazines, nude church-goers, and profane language, will serve as fuel for the fire... For I declare by Him Who made the Sun, Moon and Stars and the Habitable Earth for His home. By Whom everything was Created and Himself not Created, from infinite eternity...

Now let me go back to deal with **Revelation 20:** In this particular warning book, John of Patmos (Yakub) warns us how his people would be held in check for

1000 years before they'd be let loose to deceive the entire nations of earth. *"20 **And I saw an angel coming down out of heaven**, having the key to the Abyss and holding in his hand a great chain. ²He seized the dragon, that ancient serpent, who is the devil, or Satan, and bound him for a thousand years. ³He threw him into the Abyss, and locked and sealed it over him, **to keep him from deceiving the nations anymore until the thousand years were ended**. After that, he must be set free for a short time."*

This 1000 year period represents year 1492, the year Muslims from Mecca and North Africa lost control over Spain and the seven seas to Western Europe i.e., Caucasian Christians and Caucasian Jews. History tells us:

"January 2 – Fall of Granada: Muhammad XIII, the last Moorish Emir of Granada, surrenders his city to the army of the Catholic Monarchs, Ferdinand and Isabella, after a lengthy siege, ending the 10-year Granada War and the centuries-long Reconquista and bringing an end to 780 years of Muslim control in Al-Andalus.

"Christopher Columbus is in Alhambra, and sees the Moorish king come out of the city gates and kiss the hands of the Spanish king, queen and prince."[34]

Mathematically speaking, 1492 – 1000 = years 492 BC. Any fine historian knows Europe, in 472 BC or 492 BC, consisted of wild barbaric and vigorous tribes. For example, the Celts were a liking for single combat, after which the victor proudly displays the severed

---

[34] http://en.wikipedia.org/wiki/1492

head of his opponent.[35] Other ancient tribes were Scythians, Goths, Vandals, Teutones and Cimbri. By year 1492 the savage tribes of Europe were reorganized into five major Countries; namely, England, France, Ireland, Portugal, Spain, Scotland and Ireland.

Fundamentally speaking, *Revelations 20:1-3* symbolically hid how an amalgamation of Western European tribes would be let loose to conquer. But first they were to be delayed by the **symbolic angel (Muslims)** who came down from **heaven (Mecca)**, then set them free with the keys of government to deceive for a short time.

[Revelation 20:7-10] *"⁷ **When the thousand years (1000 years) are over, Satan will be released from his prison** ⁸ and will go out **to deceive the nations in the four corners of the earth—Gog and Magog—and to gather them for battle.** In number they are like the sand on the seashore. ⁹ They marched across the breadth of the earth and surrounded the camp of God's people, the city he loves. But fire came down from heaven and devoured them. ¹⁰ And the devil, who deceived them, was thrown into the lake of burning sulfur, where the beast and the false prophet had been thrown. They will be tormented day and night forever and ever."*

It has been 521 years [1492 – 2013] since Western Caucasians—**Gog and Magog**—has been exercising the keys of government, most deceitfully. Six more years equal 600.

No matter what, Revelation 20 symbolically ends speaking about the removal of the two opposites by the

---

[35] https://en.wikipedia.org/wiki/Hallstatt_culture

Supreme Wisdom of God Himself. *"¹¹ Then I saw a great white throne and him who was seated on it. The earth and the heavens fled from his presence, and there was no place for them."* You can gain more insight yourself by going online and read The Final Call.[36]

I pray Allah shall give you the light of understanding of the time and what is being fulfilled because the idea behind Yakub's civilization is at its wits end. This vile world has not the nature or politics to bring unity of opposites in the east, west, north or south. And all opposition against Allah's wisdom has no place to go. The party is over....

Recommended Books

www.ingramcontent.com/pod-product-compliance
Lightning Source LLC
Chambersburg PA
CBHW070608290526
45790CB00002B/826